Tottenham Walks

Tottenham Walks

*Explore Tottenham's hidden history
through four walks.*

Mareeni Raymond
and Edward Richards

Matador
9 Priory Business Park,
Wistow Road, Kibworth Beauchamp,
Leicestershire. LE8 0RX
Tel: 0116 279 2299
Email: books@troubador.co.uk
Web: www.troubador.co.uk/matador
Twitter: @matadorbooks

ISBN 978 1785899 140

British Library Cataloguing in Publication Data.
A catalogue record for this book is available from the British Library.

Printed and bound by CPI Group (UK) Ltd, Croydon, CR0 4YY
Typeset in 11pt Minion Pro by Troubador Publishing Ltd, Leicester, UK

Matador is an imprint of Troubador Publishing Ltd

For our lovely Eleanor

Foreword

We decided to write this book because we love walking in Tottenham. Ed was brought up in Tottenham and has always been a dedicated supporter of the local football team, his dedication taking him around England, Europe and beyond. Over the years he has lived in other parts of London and the world, before meeting Mareeni back in Tottenham in his thirties. Since living together in Tottenham, we've enjoyed discovering its nuances and its hidden treasures. It is a fascinating place to explore and a brilliant place to live in, and so, with our daughter in tow, we've developed four guided walks highlighting some of our favourite places and interesting facts. There are of course plenty of things we have left out, as there just isn't enough space to include everything, but we hope your interest will be piqued enough to do some further exploring yourself!

Tottenham has a very long history. It even appears in the Domesday book (1086). We know that it started off as large fields and farmland with a small village at its centre and was most likely a farming community initially. Tottenham High Road was first laid by the Romans and was known as Ermine Street. By the sixteenth century many wealthy Londoners had holiday homes in Tottenham, and Bruce Castle is the last of such homes still standing, acting as a reminder of this bygone era.

In the nineteenth century the building of roads and railways resulted in more residential areas being developed around London, and the population of Tottenham doubled between 1811 and 1851. The Great Eastern Railway opened in 1872, providing a link from Bethnal Green to Edmonton, and many of today's buildings in Tottenham can be traced back to around this time. The introduction of cheap morning train tickets helped cement Tottenham as a place for workers to reside.

Those who have never been to Tottenham may know about it through press coverage. It is a place name recognisable in many parts of the world with negative connotations as it was the starting point of the more recent riots in 2011, and an earlier riot in 1985. It may also be known for its social issues such as inequalities and housing shortages, problems that affect many parts of the country but are especially noticeable in London. However, Tottenham is also home to a hotch potch of interesting, creative, hard-working people, with a multitude of ethnicities, religions, football supporters, pub-goers and families, working towards a brilliant and thriving community atmosphere. There are many community groups, whose work has helped inform our walks, such as Friends of Tottenham Marshes, Friends of Lordship Rec, Friends of Bruce Castle Park, The Antwerp Arms, Haringey Friends of Parks, Radical History Network of North East London, Haringey Council, Bruce Castle Museum, Summerhill Road's website team, Hornsey Historical Society, and Edmonton Hundred Historical Society. We've selected recent and distant history in the book according to our own interests and what we think is important, but our aim has always been to give people an insight into the hidden beauty and history of the area and to inspire curiosity as well as pride as you walk through Tottenham – an underestimated area which we believe is one of London's best kept secrets. Please note that the maps are very simplified and not to scale so you may wish to bring your own more detailed maps with you on your adventures in Tottenham.

WALKS COVER:

1. Parks and Marshes: A pretty walk which takes you to Markfield Park's beam engine and the hidden urban garden of the Lea Valley.
2. Hidden Tottenham: From Northumberland Park to Bruce Grove, a short walk for those curious about the hidden history of the High Road.
3. Bruce Grove to Seven Sisters: A walk through the beautiful village-esque Bruce Castle area to the Broadwater Farm estate with stops along Tottenham's historical High Road and Bruce Grove.
4. Seven Sisters to St. Ann's: A short stroll exploring some of the main historical sites of Tottenham High Road and the residential West Green area.

*Authors Ed, Mareeni and their
daughter Eleanor.*

WALK 1:

Parks and Marshes

~

Start: South Tottenham overground station
Finish: Tottenham Hale station
3 Miles

~

A pretty walk which takes you to Markfield Park's beam engine and the hidden urban garden of the Lea Valley

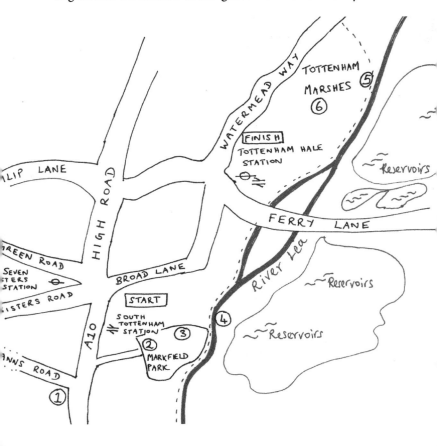

Starting from South Tottenham overground station turn left onto the High Road. Keep heading south until you see the imposing towers of *St. Ignatius church* on the right, at the junction with St Ann's Road. This Roman Catholic Church is a huge cruciform Grade II listed building with twin east towers, which dates from between 1894 and 1902. The Romanesque building, designed by Father Benedict Williamson in a late 12th Century transitional style, is so tall that it can be seen from many spots throughout South Tottenham. Filmmaker Alfred Hitchcock went to school at the nearby St Ignatius College and his family were parishioners at the church between 1910 and 1913. It is said that Hitchcock's film Vertigo was inspired by the dominant church towers.

Turn round and head north back towards South Tottenham station until you get to Gladesmore Road on the right hand side. Walk to the end of Gladesmore Road where you will find the gates to *Markfield Park*, a small local park and home to the famous *Markfield Park beam engine* which pumped sewage in the area continuously until 1988. The beam engine, seven-foot high and twenty-one foot long, is housed in the big glass windowed *original pump house*. If you really want to appreciate this impressive beam engine in action, go along on any bank holiday Monday,

Markfield Park Beam Engine

which are Steam days. Steaming goes on for a few hours on these days (for an up to date timetable, go to *http://www.mbeam.org/*). It is also open on some Sundays, and there are friendly local guides around on those days to answer your questions. In action, the sound and the steam combined are a powerful experience. The cast iron wheel and columns are beautiful and you will notice the leaf designs on the Doric style columns. (Doric is one of three ancient Greek styles of architecture typified by simple circular capitals at the top of columns). The engine was built by Wood Brothers, of Sowerby Bridge, Yorkshire, between 1886 and 1888. It was used until 1964. It is a compound rotative free-standing engine with 100 horse power, driving two pumps.

Leave via the gates just to the east of the beam engine to find yourself on a stretch of the *River Lea*. Turn left along the river to enjoy a peaceful stroll on the path, with resident birds and barges. Although be warned that on pleasant days, cyclists and joggers can make it very busy.

The River Lea

The River Lea is a natural river which runs from Hertfordshire past Stratford and down to the Thames. Although sometimes spelt Lee, it is generally agreed that the river is spelt Lea and the navigation is known as the River Lee Navigation. This part of the river forms the boundary between Tottenham (Haringey) and Waltham Forest. Continue under the bridge at Ferry Lane until you come to *Stonebridge Lock* and the *Waterside Cafe*. The remains of the original wooden lock complete with an official River Lee Trust miller's post were discovered under the house.[iii] We know that Stonebridge Lock has existed since at least 1780 as there are records of its renovation from this time. Like other locks as far as Ponder's End Lock further along, it is large enough to take barges of up to 130 tons.

From here, take the left path to enter the west side of *Tottenham Marshes* (the other half of Tottenham Marshes is located on the east side of the River Lea in Waltham Forest). Follow the path round to the left. These marshes form part of the Lea Valley, a large area of wetlands and marshes, interesting for their urban wildness. You will walk through wildflower meadows and may see bee orchid and wall bedstraw from May to June as well as kingfishers and sand martins. For detailed guided walks it is worth contacting the Friends of Tottenham Marshes, who

A butterfly spotted at Tottenham Marshes

organise regular walks exploring the history and wildlife of the marshes.[iv] Visit their website for more information: *http://www.tottenhammarshes.org/*

And for those who wish to explore the Lea valley further, many walks are described at *https://www.visitleevalley.org.uk/*

Walk through the marshes back towards Tottenham Hale (with the river on your left). As you walk back towards Tottenham Hale note that on Ferry Lane, the largest furniture factory in the world once stood and many thousands of employees travelled to and lived around this bustling site. Harris Lebus built the factory in 1900 and the name became synonymous with good quality furniture built using the latest technology at the time. During World Wars I and II it was temporarily used to build munitions. In the sixties the site was sold to the Greater London council and became a housing estate and storage facility.[vvi]

After walking past some allotments you will exit the marshes on Ferry Lane. Turn right and you're back at Tottenham Hale station. Alternatively, if you fancy the more scenic (and longer) walk, head north from the Waterside Cafe at Stonebridge Lock into the marshes and walk to the exit just to the east of Northumberland Park station. The station is less than five minutes' walk (across a busy road and over a railway footbridge) and is where walk 2 starts.

FOOD AND DRINK

- Waterside Cafe at Stonebridge Lock (Watermead Way, London N17 0XD) located on the marshes and by the River Lea it makes a great place to start walks or cycles along the Lea Valley.
- Craving Coffee (Unit 3, Gaunson House, Markfield Road, N15 4QQ. Open 10am-5pm every day) for light lunches and hot drinks and often has evening events on Thursdays, Fridays and Saturdays.
- Markfield Park cafe, (Markfield Road, London N15 4RB. Open 9am–6pm *markfieldparkcafe.co.uk*) for sandwiches and hot drinks, in the park next to the beam engine museum.

WALK 2:

Hidden Tottenham

~

Start: Northumberland Park overground station
Finish: Bruce Grove overground station
Miles: 1.5

~

From Northumberland Park to Bruce Grove, a short walk
for those curious about the hidden history of the High Road.

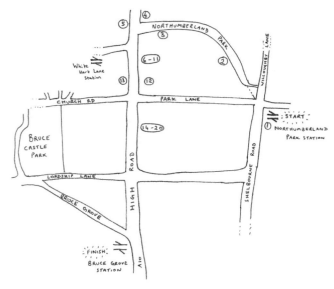

1. *Northumberland Park station*
2. *Northumberland Park estate*
3. *Walter Tull's home*
4. *816-822 High Road*

5. 810 (Holly House) and 808 High Road
6. 797 High Road (Markham Place 1829)
7. 792-802 High Road (Northumberland Terrace)
8. 796 High Road (Percy House)
9. 790 High Road (Dial House)
10. 744 Warmington House
11. 746-750 High Road (now demolished)
12. Football stadium
13. St Francis de Sales church
14. 707, Moselle House
15. 699 Tottenham Baptist Church
16. Whitbread Brewery
17. 639 High Road
18. Former carpet shop
19. 614 High Road (Former Blue School and now the Pride of Tottenham pub)
20. No 581 High Road, or Charlton House

Northumberland Park station was once called Marsh Lane station, and was opened in 1842. Initially, Tottenham Hotspur Football Club (nowadays fondly nicknamed Spurs) played at Asplins Farm, beside the railway line in Northumberland Park, before moving a short distance to White Hart Lane stadium in 1899. Confusingly, the stadium is not actually on White Hart Lane, but on the High Road. From the station, turn left (away from the railway tracks) and cross the road. Veer to the right and cut through the small bus station until you turn left onto Northumberland Park. As you walk along Northumberland Park you will catch sight of large Victorian villas harking back to a time when this area was very affluent, now almost hidden by the 1970s built, council owned, *Northumberland Park estate.* The estate is earmarked for substantial regeneration over the next decade or two.

Approximately halfway up Northumberland Park, on the right hand side and on the corner of Grange Road, you'll see a block of flats on which there is a blue plaque, indicating the site of the former house where *Walter Tull* once lived. Walter Tull played for Tottenham Hotspur between 1909 and 1911, and then for Northampton Town, and became the first black officer in the British Army during the First World War. The plaque was installed by the Nubian Jak Community Trust in 2014.[vii] In his biography[viii] the author describes Tull's incredible achievements despite the racism endured both on and off the football pitch throughout his life.

Continue on to the busy High Road, and to the North of Northumberland Park (towards Edmonton) you will see some *Georgian buildings (816/818, 820, and 822 High Road)* which at the time of writing had been earmarked for North Tottenham Heritage Restoration works as part of lottery funded improvements. Heading back south down the High Road you will see two *Grade II* listed Georgian buildings. 810 High Road (Holly House)* and its partner *808* were built around 1715-20 and are outstanding early examples of a pair of Queen Anne style early Georgian houses, symmetrical, and flanked by coach house wings. As Grade II* listed buildings they rank amongst the 6% most important buildings listed nationally. Notice the narrow windows at each end, blind windows of the central shared wall, and the dark red brick. Spot the differences between the two buildings, mainly due to their restoration being completed at different times and by different teams.

Continue south along the High Road and you will get to *792-802 High Road* which were once known as

808-810 High Road

Northumberland Terrace. The site previously belonged to the Percy family, Dukes of Northumberland. Sir Henry Percy was commonly known as Harry Hotspur, hence Tottenham Hotspur football club – the name was actually chosen by a group of boys who had grown up in Northumberland Park and wanted the name to reflect the area's history in some way. These mid 18th century three storey buildings are huge houses, with impressive Doric entrances, set back from the road and built with yellow London stock brick with red brick dressings.

No 796 is *Percy House*, a Grade II* listed building which was built 1750-52 by Robert Plimpton, a timber merchant. Percy House is now owned by Spurs. Percy House is on English Heritage's 'at risk' register. Its front boundary wall, railings, and ornamental gates are also listed Grade II*. In May 2015 Spurs announced that Percy House is to be the new long-term home of the Tottenham Hotspur Foundation, a charitable arm of the football club which does work in the local community.

Number 790 is *Dial House*, a Grade II* listed building with a sun dial and '1691' on the side wall because it was built that year by Moses Trulock, a city soap manufacturer. The Trulock family owned the building until the 1830s. It was restored in the 1980s as flats. The southern wall was rebuilt as part of the Spurs development.

As you continue south down the High Road you will see where there were, until very recently, three more historic buildings, 746, 748, and 750 High Road. These were approved for demolition as part of the planning application for the new Tottenham Hotspur stadium. Number 750 was previously the *White Hart pub* built in the late 19th century. Number 748 was *The Red House*, originally a coffee house built around 1878-80 and *number 746* was built in 1910 on the site of an older 1864 building which provided free or cheap medical help for the poor.

Number 744, known as *Warmington House*, is another Georgian building built in 1828, and was originally to be demolished as part of the Spurs redevelopment project, but will now remain after significant objections were received. It is to be retained and incorporated into a new terrace with a museum called "The Tottenham Experience". It was named after James Warmington, a farmer and coal merchant, and was occupied in 1888 by J.A Prestwich who was a famous engineer and pioneer in the development of cinematography projectors, cameras, and motorcycle engines.

While walking along the High Road you can't miss the *football stadium*. The original stadium was known as White Hart Lane and built in 1899. Although it had a much larger capacity back when football stadiums had terraces (the highest attendance recorded at White Hart Lane was when Tottenham Hotspur played Sunderland in March 1938 in front of 75,038 supporters), the final capacity of White Hart Lane was 36,284.

Warmington House and the Spurs ground being reconstructed in the background

In order to compete with the big clubs in the Premier League, Spurs knew they needed a bigger stadium and obtained permission for a new 61,000 seat stadium, complete with new flats, a museum, hotel, and extreme sports centre.

The new stadium will be built next to the existing one (in fact the North stand of the current ground will be the South stand of the new stadium). At the time of writing construction is already underway.

The *Church of St Francis de Sales* is opposite the stadium and is a local listed building. It is an attractive Roman Catholic Church built in 1895 designed by Sinnott, Sinnott, and Powell, dominated by a large arched window and a stone cross. It is adjoined to the rear by a locally listed

St Francis de Sales Church

Moselle House

school building which was constructed in 1882. Number 729 High Road is the church presbytery, a grand locally listed Victorian villa.

Number 707, Moselle House, is another admirable three storey early 19th Century Grade II listed building identifiable by the oval plaque at second floor level inscribed 'MOSELLE HOUSE'. Moselle is the name of the river that runs through Tottenham and the name comes from "Mossy hill" which became Muswell Hill and was one of the sources of the river. The river runs through Tottenham Cemetery, Lordship Rec, and even under Coombes Croft Library on the High Road

Tottenham Baptist Church

13

just north of Moselle House, where a glass panel in the floor allows you to (just about) see the river flowing underneath.

Number 699 High Road is the *Tottenham Baptist Church*, built in 1825 by Joseph Fletcher. You will see four imposing Doric columns at the front and a Venetian style window. The church was restored in the 1990s and is now floodlit at night. Inside the church there is an upstairs gallery running round the inside on three sides of the church, with restored cast iron railings and gates with unusual box section piers.

Whitbread Brewery

Whitbread Brewery is an interesting looking building at 676 High Road, which has a Grade II listed former southern gate building, a central square clock-tower, and cornice incised 'BREWERY'.

Next is the *former Carpet shop (currently a Sports Direct) at 636-638 High Road*, which was burnt down in the 2011 riots. On Thursday 4 August 2011, a police officer shot and killed 29-year-old Mark Duggan during a targeted vehicle stop procedure on the Ferry Lane bridge next to Tottenham Hale station, sparking outrage in some quarters. Subsequently, an at first peaceful march on Saturday 6 August in Tottenham was followed by rioting and looting, first in Tottenham, then across London and, later in the week, other parts of the UK. The documentary film "The Hard Stop" directed by George Amponsah is about the riots and the tensions between the police and black and other minority communities at the time and afterwards.[ix]

On the opposite side of the High Road is *Number 639 High Road*, a neo-Jacobean style Grade II listed building that was also heavily damaged in the riots but retained far more of its original features. Built in 1901 as the offices of Tottenham and Edmonton Gas Company by John Sherwell Corder and extended in 1914, this Edwardian building has several stained glass windows and Art Nouveau patterns throughout, with elaborate turrets. It is now owned by the Greater London

Number 639 High Road

Authority and is an Enterprise Centre managed by the London Youth Support Trust which helps local people get started in business and gain employment skills.[x]

614 High Road is the site of the former *Blue Coat School*, a school for girls built in 1833, which is now The Pride of Tottenham pub. The school was named because of the colour of the school uniforms.

The former Blue Coat School

Continue heading south along the High Road until you see three impressive Georgian houses on the other side of the road, numbers 581 to 585 (odd). Charlton Cottage, *Number 581 High Road*, is a Grade II listed two storey building, built in 1750 and now a doctor's surgery. The main entrance has a six panelled door in a painted stone doorcase with Tuscan style columns.

From here you can continue South to Bruce Grove station or keep going to get to Seven Sisters underground station.

FOOD AND DRINK

The Beehive Pub (Stoneleigh Road, N17 9BQ | TEL: 020 8808 3567. *beehiven17.com*) a pub just off the High Road not too far Bruce Grove station with a good range of ales, outside space, and serving hot food.

WALK 3:

Bruce Grove to Seven Sisters

~

Start: Bruce Grove overground station
Finish: Seven Sisters station
Miles: 3.5 miles

~

A walk through the beautiful village-esque Bruce Castle area to the Broadwater farm estate with stops along Tottenham's historical High Road and Bruce Grove.

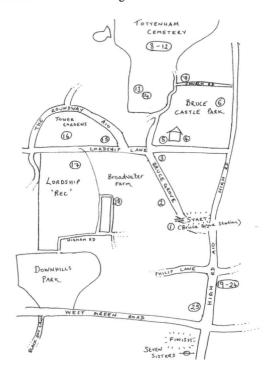

1. *Bruce Grove station*
2. *7 Bruce Grove (Luke Howard's home)*
3. *Edmanson's Close (The almshouses)*
4. *Bruce Castle*
5. *The Tower*
6. *Bruce Castle Park Oak Tree*
7. *The Antwerp Arms*
8. *Tottenham Cemetery*
9. *Chapels*
10. *War memorial*
11. *Bernie Grant's grave*
12. *All Hallows Church*
13. *The Priory*
14. *Peabody cottages*
15. *Tower Gardens Conservation area*
16. *Lordship recreation ground*
17. *Broadwater Farm Estate*
18. *Bernie Grant Arts Centre*
19. *Victorian swimming baths*
20. *Town Hall*
21. *Memorial to Cynthia Jarrett*
22. *Tottenham War Memorial*
23. *Old fire station*
24. *Old Jewish hospital*
25. *Seven Sisters station*

Bruce Grove Station was opened in 1872 by the Great Eastern Railway on the route from Liverpool Street to Enfield. In the early 1980s the station was modernised but was more recently reconstructed in the original style. In November 2015 planning permission was granted to turn the station into "a landmark spacious building with a striking copper-coloured steel facade."[xi]

From Bruce Grove station, turn left to reach *7 Bruce Grove*, which features an English Heritage blue plaque for Luke Howard (1772–1864), the meteorologist known as the *Father of meteorology* for his detailed observations over many years of the weather and cloud formations in Tottenham. He proposed a classification and nomenclature of the clouds in 1802 and published his findings in *'On the Modification of Clouds'* in 1803. His daily barometric pressure readings are among the earliest consistent scientific observations recorded.[xii] The Cloud Appreciation Society and Tottenham Clouds[xiii] maintain a website about Luke Howard, his home and his work, and his home will hopefully be restored in future.

There are a number of grand old houses along the southern side of Bruce Grove, giving an indication of Tottenham's former days as a retreat for the wealthy escaping London.

On the northern side of Bruce Grove, as you approach Lordship Lane and Bruce Castle Park, you will pass *Edmanson's Close*, built in 1870 'for the poor, elderly people of Tottenham and Bow'[xiv] by the Drapers Company to replace three almshouses in the City. The architect was Herbert Williams. Almshouses were charitable housing provided to enable, usually older, retired people, to live at low cost. The almshouses are surrounded by picturesque gardens.

Edmanson's Close, formerly almshouses

When you get to the end of Bruce Grove you'll see the entrance to Bruce Castle Park and the magnificent Grade 1 listed Tudor former manor house of *Bruce Castle* itself.

Bruce Castle Museum

At the time of the Norman Conquest the medieval manor house on the site of today's Bruce Castle was the seat of the

Manor of Tottenham. The manor reached the River Lea in the east; and in the west to today's Alexandra Palace (formerly Tottenham Wood) and belonged to Waltheof and Judith, the Earl and Countess of Huntingdon (her name is recorded in the Domesday Book in 1086). Their daughter Maud married David, King of Scotland. Eventually, the manor passed to the De Bruce family – the last of whom was famously Robert the Bruce, when he became King of Scotland. Look out for statues of David and Maud who feature later in this walk at All Hallows Church. The present house dates from the early sixteenth century. It is known that Henry VIII visited as well as Elizabeth I. The building was used as a refuge from the Plague in the 1500s. The architectural designs and interiors of the surviving building date mainly from the 17th and 18th centuries, under the Lords Coleraine.

In 1827 the house became Bruce Castle School, headed by Rowland Hill and his brother Arthur. The Hill family's school was well-known for its progressive teaching methods (no corporal punishment, for instance). Charles Dickens visited it many times. The school continued until 1890. Sir Rowland Hill became famous for inventing the Penny Post system in 1840. Bruce Castle is now the local history museum and archive. If you wish to see Haringey's past from the Romans onwards, enjoy art exhibitions or view original historic documents about the area, it is worth visiting (Bruce Castle Museum, Lordship Lane, London, N17 8NU. Check *www.haringey.gov.uk/brucecastlemuseum* for current opening hours and events).

The Tudor Tower to the left has been a matter of speculation as to its original purpose for many years. Recent research suggests it was possibly built to house falcons. Today you may see local artists' exhibitions or similar events inside the Tower.

The oak tree in Bruce Castle Park

To the right of the castle there is a path, follow this path and continue straight through the park, past the play area on the left and a huge *oak tree* on the right. This tree is more than 500 years old. Tottenham Trees[xv] (*http://www.tottenhamtrees. org*) is a branch of the Charter for Trees, Woods and People (which at the time of writing will be launched in 2017) and their aim is to ensure trees are respected and that Tottenham continues to grow and maintain trees and green spaces. Their website is a good resource for information on all tree-related activities and history in Tottenham, including the story of the Seven Sisters trees.

The path then veers left where you may exit through the gate and turn right to follow the road round the park or continue walking straight through the park towards the *Antwerp Arms pub*,[xvi] open since 1822 and now north London's first ever community-owned pub.

The Antwerp Arms, a community run pub

Following the modern bustle of the High Road this tranquil stretch of conservation area seems like a different world – you could be walking through a fancy part of a countryside village. Just to the left (if facing the pub) is a small pathway called Prospect Place, with pretty houses on the right side.

Prospect Place

Tottenham Cemetery. Walk to the far end of the cemetery to see Moselle Lake and its wildlife.

Walk down this path until you see the gates on the left to *Tottenham cemetery*, another peaceful conservation area in Tottenham which was first opened in 1857, and has been extended since. Many first and second World War graves are here, and some are unmarked. You'll see the beautiful *chapels* ahead. The two chapels were designed by George Pritchett in 1856 and are non-conformist in style, joined together by a bellcote and a central arched carriageway. The late 19th century stained glass windows in the west of one of the chapels shows the resurrection, and other stained glass windows also remain.[xvii]

Look out for a grade II listed little bridge and tunnel near the chapel. Follow the path round to the left and continue on it as it loops round, past a white stone *Second World War memorial* on both sides of the path and then *Bernie Grant's grave.*

Bernie Grant was a labour MP for Tottenham from 1987 until his death in 2000 during which time he was a popular,

War memorial in Tottenham Cemetery

but sometimes controversial character. This quote from his obituary in the Guardian summarises this well: "A black man with a leftwing trade union background, he was also an anti-apartheid campaigner, a supporter of revolutionary governments, feminist causes, black studies and a multi-racial school curriculum. He became the figurehead and tireless activist in cases of official harassment or misconduct, notably the Joy Gardner case, where a black woman died after immigration officers entered her house and put her under restraint. And in 1985 when a riot exploded on Tottenham's Broadwater Farm estate and a policeman, Keith Blakelock, was murdered, Bernie commented that the youths on the estate felt that the police had received "a bloody good hiding." The remark made him a notorious hate figure in the pages of the tabloids."[xviii]

Continue down the path to exit the cemetery and reach *All Hallows Anglican Church*, one of the oldest churches in London, built in 1150. John Constable's painting of the church "All Hallows Church – Tottenham" is now in

New York's Metropolitan Museum of Art.

All Hallows Church

The building has been updated over the centuries but some of the original building can be seen. The tower is the oldest part, dating back to the 14th and 15th centuries. There are eight bells. In 1876, a parishioner, Mr. Butterfield, restored parts of the church so it looked more Victorian in style.[xix] He is buried in the adjacent Tottenham Cemetery. Many of the stained glass windows originate from this Victorian update. Look for two windows at the Eastern end of

Left: Stained glass windows inside All Hallows Church
Right: A Celtic cross in the churchyard

Left: The statue of Maud at All Hallows Church
Right: The Grade II* listed Priory gates

the church. These are 16th or 17th century Flemish or French windows and are stunning. Go round to the main entrance of the church and at the door of the church there are two small sculptures on either side. One, added in the 1930s, is of King David I of Scotland, who is said to have given Tottenham the church. On the other side is a sculpture of Maud, his wife.

Next door to the church is the *Grade II* listed Priory*, with an 18th century iron gate. It has been the vicarage since 1906 and was previously a farmhouse.

Continue past the Priory and eventually you'll turn right onto busy Lordship Lane. On the right, are the *Peabody Cottages*, built between 1903 and 1907. These formed one of the first two estates that Peabody built which contained houses as opposed to flats. The Peabody Cottages can only be entered and exited via two roads off Lordship Lane and, as they look quite similar to homes on the Tower Garden

Examples of homes on the Peabody estate

estate it is not essential to take a detour to see them, although the history which surrounds George Peabody and his desire to provide poor Londoners with good quality housing is very interesting and seems all the more relevant today with Londoners experiencing a very real housing crisis.

You'll find Bennington Road on your right. From this road turn left onto Tower Gardens Road. This is the oldest part of the *Tower Gardens Estate*, built from 1903 onwards. The estate occupies a special place in history as one of the world's first garden suburbs. It consists of low rise mainly residential buildings, with high architectural standards built specifically for working class people formerly living in overcrowded homes in Tower Hamlets (hence 'Tower Gardens').

Keep walking until you can turn left down Waltheof Avenue, across Lordship Lane and into *Lordship recreation ground*, a remnant of Tottenham's previous open countryside; the earliest map of the Tottenham area was produced by the Earl of Dorset in 1619 showing that the areas of Downhills,

Broad Waters and Lordsmeade were what is now Lordship Recreation Ground, fondly referred to locally as "The Rec".

Lordship Recreation ground, with Broadwater Farm estate in the background

The Rec opened in 1936 and was redeveloped in 2012. It has been improved through campaigns by Lordship Rec Users

Lordship Recreation ground, where plenty of wildlife can be seen around the Moselle River and lake

Forum (LRUF) and Friends of Lordship Rec[xx] and is now very popular with local families, especially the main community building, "The Hub" which has thriving community support and activities and is run by locals and volunteers. The Hub was built in an eco-friendly way with the help of volunteers, using straw bales, wood and natural clay. The Rec is a beautiful and large area to explore, and includes conservation areas, wildlife habitats, an open air theatre shaped like a shell, built in 1936 (The Shell Theatre), and a model traffic area built in 1938, which used to be a spot for children to learn about navigating roads (it even had traffic lights!) and is now used mainly by cyclists. There is plenty of detailed history on the Friends of Lordship Rec website (*http://lordshiprec.org.uk*). As you walk through the ground look left to see *Broadwater Farm estate*, a large housing estate which was originally a farm in 1798. It is called Broadwater because the area used to flood before the culverting of the river. Building of Broadwater Farm estate started in 1967 and was a massive development of high density housing with initially 1063 flats to house 3000-4000 people. The architects were C E Jacobs and later Alan Weitzel who were the borough architects. The blocks, named after World War II airfields, were connected by walkways. By 1981 a process of refurbishment had started but progress was slow.

The Broadwater Farm estate is known for the riot of 6 October 1985. Tensions were high after Dorothy 'Cherry' Groce was shot accidentally during a police search for her son, in Brixton. Soon afterwards, Cynthia Jarrett, died due to heart failure during a police search in her home near Broadwater Farm, and the riot ensued, resulting in many injured and the death of a policeman. After the riot a £33 million redevelopment project took place.

Broadwater Farm estate

You can enter the estate through the park. On Rochford block, to the east of Debden block and only visible from within the estate, is the Peace Mural by Anthony Steele in 1987, showing Martin Luther King, Ghandi, Bob Marley and John Lennon in a garden setting with children playing. Also within the estate is the Garden of Remembrance, south of Tangmer block, which commemorates Cynthia Jarrett and Keith Blakelock, with the wider struggle symbolised by the rocks rising out of the ground. There is also a huge waterfall mural of Dunn's Waterfall in Jamaica by B Hall and D Taylor from 1991 on the southern wall of Debden block.

Exit the estate by heading south along Willan Road until you can turn left onto The Avenue. Keep going until you get to Mount Pleasant Road on the right hand side. Walk down Mount Pleasant Road, past some examples of larger Victorian and Edwardian homes until you get to Philip Lane. Turn left and then right at Jansons Road. There are some pretty cottages here and at the end of the road is Clyde Circus, effectively a residential roundabout. Go left around the circus and take the second left which will take you over a bridge and to the back of the leisure centre. Turn right and walk to the back of the *Bernie Grant Arts Centre (BGAC)*.[xxi] Ahead of you is the old fire station workers' cottages, now residences managed by a housing association. Turn left to come around the side of *BGAC*, a £15 million purpose-built multi-arts centre. The centre was designed by David Adjaye and opened in September 2007. There is purpleheart wood in the foyer, specially imported from Guyana because that was where Bernie Grant was born. The centre was built on the site of a former *Victorian swimming baths*, and you can see a plaque explaining the original use of the building on its frontage as you exit onto Tottenham Town Hall Approach Road. This section of Tottenham Green is lined by baroque grand Grade II listed Edwardian public buildings, constructed between 1904 and 1905 by A. S. Tayler and R Jemmett on the sites of large 18th Century houses.

Next door is the Grade II Listed former *Town Hall* which opened in November 1905, and was also built by the borough architects A S Taylor and A R Jemmett. The style is Edwardian baroque and reminiscent of 17th century Dutch architecture, in brick with stone accents. It is worth exploring inside; the mosaic-floored foyer is on two levels, leading to the staircase branching up to the landing. Balusters are stone, the handrails dark marble, and the walls have complex panelling and window-framing. The stained glass is Renaissance in style. The Moselle Room has a Moorish-Jacobean style ceiling. Refurbishment of the town hall (now known as the 'Dream Centre') was completed in 2011.

Town Hall Approach Road with the Town Hall and the former swimming baths, now part of Bernie Grant Arts Centre.

Outside the town hall is a discreet stone memorial on the ground, which is a *memorial to Cynthia Jarrett,* the Afro-Caribbean lady referred to earlier, whose death during a police search at her home triggered the Broadwater Farm riot in 1985.

At the southern end of Town Hall Approach Road, at its junction with the High Road, is the Grade II* listed *Tottenham War Memorial,* which was erected in 1923.

Continue walking south down the High Road to see a red-bricked large building on the right called Sycamore gardens, which was once a

A blue plaque on the Town Hall dedicated to Bernie Grant

33

Hospital or "Home for Jewish incurables". In 1913 the home was further extended and a synagogue designed by Marcus Collins, who had also designed the Home, was opened in 1914. The home closed in 1995 and was later converted into social housing.

A few yards further you will arrive at the end of this walk, at Seven Sisters station.

FOOD AND DRINK

- Chicken Town (The Old Fire Station, Town Hall Approach Road, London N15 4RX. chicken-town. co.uk) a social enterprise which aims to use sales from meals to subsidise the provision of cheap "healthy" fried chicken to young people as an alternative to really unhealthy fried chicken places on the High Road. It has proved very popular with some while others are critical about offering any form of fried chicken, even if much healthier than competitors.
- The Hub, Lordship Recreation Ground, London, N17 6NU. *www.lordshiphub.org.uk* for drinks, snacks and lunch.
- The Antwerp Arms (Antwerp Arms, 168-170 Church Rd, London N17 8AS. *http://www.antwerparms. co.uk/*) This is a community owned pub, saved through members of the community coming together and buying shares in the pub. There are regular shareholder meetings ensuring that the community has a real say in how it is run.

WALK 4

Seven Sisters to St. Ann's

~

Start: Seven Sisters station
Finish: Green Lanes (either Turnpike Lane underground
station or Harringay Green Lanes overground station)
3 miles

~

A short stroll exploring some of the main historical sites
of Tottenham High Rd and the residential West Green
area.

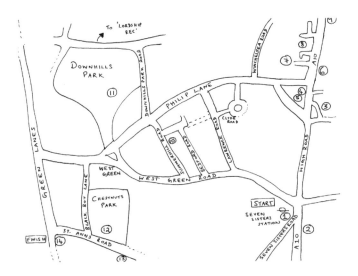

1. *Seven Sisters*
2. *Page Green Terrace*
3. *Former Deaconesses hospital*

4. *Holy Trinity Church*
5. *Old well*
6. *Tottenham High Cross*
7. *High Cross Girls School*
8. *The former Palace Theatre of Varieties*
9. *Police station*
10. *Summerhill Road*
11. *Downhills Park*
12. *Chestnuts*
13. *St Ann's Hospital*
14. *The Salisbury Pub*

Starting at *Seven Sisters* station, walk to *Page Green Terrace*. Seven Sisters is named after a circle of seven elms, likely to have been originally planted around the 14th century at Page Green, as shown on the Earl of Dorset's survey of 1619. There are various myths and legends surrounding the history of the trees. However, we know that seven new trees were planted by the seven daughters of a Mr. J McRae in 1852 and replanted in 1886 by another set of seven sisters. Since then the tradition of replanting the trees in a circle when they need replacing has continued. One of the spades used by the sisters in 1886 is in Bruce Castle museum. Walking north from the station turn right onto the busy Broad Lane and then left onto Talbot Road, a quiet street fronted by Victorian, Edwardian and late 20th century residences. An example is the very pretty No. 41 Spring Cottage, a two storey Grade II listed Victorian villa. Between the door and first floor window is a painted stone plaque inscribed 'Spring Cottage 1857'. Numbers 1 to 19 (odd) Talbot Road form a consistent terrace of late 19th century two storey Edwardian dwellings.

At the end of the road turn left and then immediately right onto Tottenham Green East, which used to be called Hospital Common, for the Evangelical Protestant Deaconesses Institution and Training Hospital, established in 1868. This became Tottenham Hospital in 1899 and in 1907 it was re-named the Prince of Wales General Hospital, which closed in the 1980s. It is now a block of flats called *Deaconess Court*.

Deaconess Court

The end of this road brings you back to the busy High Road, and if you cross over and continue north you will see *Holy Trinity church*, a Grade II* listed church built between 1828 and 1830 to designs by James Savage to meet the needs of the growing South Tottenham community at the time. Savage modelled the church on King's College Chapel, Cambridge.

Next to the church is where the High Cross Pump originally stood. A *well* was sunk in 1791 by the Lord of the Manor, Thomas Smith, to replace an earlier well to the west. In 1859 the Board of Health provided a drinking fountain with a conical roof and pump in place of the well but its water was declared to be unfit to drink in 1883, and it was subsequently

Holy Trinity Church, and the Old School House

surrounded by Art Nouveau style wrought iron railings, now Grade II listed.

Just slightly further north up the High Road, at the junction with Monument Way, is an island in the road with the *Tottenham High Cross* on it. It is now a brick column but was originally made of wood in 1600 and served as a waypoint. It was repaired and decorated in Gothic style and covered with cement in the form you see it today in 1809.[xxii]

The old well

Continue north and on the left *High Cross Girls' School* will soon become visible, set back about 20 metres

Tottenham High Cross Monument

from the High Road. Built in 1848 it was the Worshipful Company of Drapers' College for Boys until 1885, and became the girls' school in 1909. There is a plaque on the north side with a carving which was originally on the Millhouse Almshouses, which were previously located on this very site. The school is now a collection of flats, many with mezzanine levels due to the height of the original ceilings.

Continuing along the High Road you will arrive at the magnificent former *Palace Theatre of Varieties* at 421-27 Tottenham High Road. It was designed

The former Tottenham High School for Girls (later High Cross Comprehensive School)

by noted theatre architects Wylson & Long and built in 1908 in an Ionic style. Few theatres designed by these two remain, and this one is in particularly good condition. You can see the Ionic and neo-Baroque/Grecian style decoration inside and out, with gilded statues in niches inside the building. The building has been a Music Hall theatre, a cinema, bingo hall and nightclub, and now, a religious centre. If you can enter, notice the Norwegian green marble pilasters (the building is not always open to the public). There is a marble mosaic floor, which at the time of writing is sadly hidden under carpet.

The former Palace Theatre of Varieties

Further down, on the other side of the road, at 398 High Road, is the *Police Station*, an early 20th Century neo-Georgian three storey red brick building which is known for being the end point of the protest which started at Broadwater Farm estate after Duggan's death in 2011, leading to local and then national riots. It was also the starting point of the protest which preceded the riots on the Broadwater Farm estate in 1985.

Tottenham Police Station

The next part of the walk takes you through some residential streets. Go slightly further north up the High Road and turn left onto Forster Road, and then left onto Winchelsea Road, to get to Philip Lane where you turn right. At number 205 Philip Lane a corn dealer once lived and a gold "Hovis" sign was displayed on the building as seen in photos of the street from 1911.

Turn left onto Lawrence Road and then right onto the footpath opposite Clyde Road. Then turn left to get to Bedford Road, the site of some impressive old houses. Turn right at the end onto West Green Road and then right again to bring you back up to Philip Lane via *Summerhill Road*. You are now in the West Green area. This road is interesting because of the variety of houses from different periods, many detached, that you can see as you walk up it. The terraces nearer the top end of this road on the right hand side before Elizabeth Close were built between 1856 and 1859.

Turn left at the end of the road to get back onto Philip Lane. At the mini roundabout turn right onto *Downhills Park Road*. Walk up the road until you reach the entrance to Downhills Park on your left and enter the park. The park once contained a grand Georgian house, called Downhills (later Mount Pleasant House) built before 1728, at the north-east corner of the present park. Sadly, only part of the wall remains. However, as you walk through the park you can imagine the house, surrounded by 18th-century landscaped garden, with woods, a hornbeam avenue, Italian gardens, a fountain, croquet lawn, arbour, rockery and pond. Some of the 19th century garden features have been reimagined by the council and the landscaped park and atmosphere is certainly pleasant and peaceful. There are three statues as part of a park bench, representing local heroes. Have a guess at who they are! They represent

Walter Tull and Luke Howard, both mentioned in earlier walks in this book, and Olympic gold medalist Nicola Adams, who was the first woman to win an Olympic boxing title, and who trained at the Haringey Police Community Club, in High Road, Tottenham.

Exit the park through the South Entrance to see West Green. The West Green area was countryside, and then a country village

One of three sculptures in Downhills Park, this one depicting Nicola Adams

Tottenham Community Sports Centre on the High Road

until the late 1800's. It is now a popular residential area of South Tottenham connecting Tottenham to Haringey Green Lanes.

The War Memorial on West Green in front of the Harris Academy

Turn right onto West Green Road then cross the zebra crossing and go down Black Boy Lane, passing *Chestnuts park* on the left. Originally this land housed a watercress farm, a crop which thrives in wet conditions. The stream which used to run through the park is now housed in an underground station culvert. In around 1850 Chestnuts House was built in the park but eventually was demolished. Now the land is used as a recreation ground. Opposite the southern edge of the park is *St Ann's hospital*. Tottenham was the location for one of the new phase of hospitals erected by the Metropolitan Asylums Board in the 1890s. In 1892, there was an outbreak of scarlet fever, and to accommodate this, many emergency temporary buildings, originally only intended to last a year, were set up on the 19-acre site. Almost twenty years later, the 'temporary' buildings were finally made into permanent structures and it is now over 33 acres and has many different medical and administrative buildings.

Continue to walk west on St Ann's Road to arrive at the large *Salisbury pub* on Green Lanes.

The pub has a beautiful mosaic floor, worth a visit to admire. The Salisbury was originally a grand hotel built and designed by John Cathles Hill, founder of The London Brick Company. In 2003, it was restored and has become a popular local pub. Harringay Green Lanes has a very distinct identity, centred around the large number of Turkish restaurants there and the residential roads known as "the ladder" (due to how they appear on the map), but few residents associate themselves with Tottenham, even though it is officially still part of the Tottenham constituency. The above sentence was included by Ed, who is aware of the many Arsenal fans lurking around this area, unaware or unwilling to admit that they in fact live in Tottenham!

From here you can head along Green Lanes, south for Harringay Green Lanes overground station or north for Turnpike Lane underground station.

FOOD AND DRINK

- Choose one of many authentic Turkish restaurants on Green Lanes
- The Banc, (261-263 West Green Road, N15 3BH) for burgers and steaks
- The Banc Brasserie, (next to Downhills Park at 338 Philip Lane 338 Philip Lane, N15) for coffee, cake and light bites
- Both the Downhills Park community cafe and Lordship Rec community hub are in their respective parks, and are good community run cafes.
- The Salisbury pub (1 Green Lanes, St Ann's Road, London N4 1JX) has a good selection of ales

Acknowledgements

With special thanks to Deborah Hedgecock, Curator at Bruce Castle Museum, and all the staff at Haringey Archive and Museum Service; Rita and David Cottridge and the rest of the Friends of Tottenham Marshes; Joan Curtis and the Friends of Lordship Rec team; Friends of Bruce Castle Park, The Antwerp Arms; Margaret Burr and the team at Tottenham Clouds https://tottenhamclouds.org.uk); Haringey Friends of Parks (http://haringeyfriendsofparks. org.uk); Radical History Network of North East London; Haringey Council; Alan Swain and the Summerhill Road's website team (http://tottenham-summerhillroad. com); Hornsey Historical Society; Edmonton Hundred Historical Society; Joseph Nicholas and the Tottenham Civic Society team (http://www.tottenhamcivicsociety. org.uk); Glynis Kirkwood-Warren and all the other staff at The Hub, Lordship Recreation Ground; Ken Brereton and the rest of the Markfield Park beam engine team; Mustafa Suleman (http://www.harrislebus.com); our friends and families.

All photos were taken by Mareeni Raymond.

About the authors

Mareeni Raymond is a doctor working in North-East London. She has done some medical writing in the past but this is her first foray into guided walks! Ed Richards joined the Tottenham regeneration team at Haringey Council after many years of working across London in social housing related positions. Ed has degrees in both Urban Studies and Housing Practice. He is looking forward to taking his daughter to places in Tottenham that he loved as a child growing up there, such as The Model Traffic Area in Lordship Recreation ground!

References

i. Fisk, pp 20-31, F Fisk 'History of the Ancient Parish of Tottenham' 1923 (Bruce Castle Archive) pp 160-1

ii. City of Cities: The Birth of Modern London. Simon Inwood. Pan Macmillan 2007.

iii. http://www.leeandstort.co.uk/Stonebridge_Lock.htm

iv. Friends of Tottenham Marshes (http://www.tottenhammarshes.org)

v. http://www.harrislebus.com

vi. Investigating the past...the Harris Lebus Factory (Bruce Castle Museum) http://www.harrislebus.com/images/lebus.pdf

vii. Nubian Jak Community Trust. http://openplaques.org/organisations/nubian_jak

viii. Walter Tull 1888-1918 Officer Footballer: All the Guns in France Couldn't Wake Me Phil Vasili (Raw Press)

ix. The Hard Stop (documentary film by George Amponsah) 2016

x. http://www.639centre.com

xi. http://www.haringey.gov.uk/news/thumbs-stunning-bruce-grove-station-revamp

xii. The Eliot papers 1895, Quarterly Journal of the Royal Meteorological Society, Vol. XX, 1894

xiii. https://tottenhamclouds.org.uk

xiv. http://www.londongardensonline.org.uk/gardens-online-record.asp?ID=HGY012

xv. http://www.tottenhamtrees.org

xvi. www.antwerparms.co.uk

xvii. Hugh Meller, London Cemeteries, Cambridge University Press, 1981, p. 269

xviii. https://www.theguardian.com/news/2000/apr/10/guardianobituaries.obituaries

xix. English Heritage Primary Research File HAR 49; Bridget Cherry & Nikolaus Pevsner, The Buildings of England: London 4: North (Penguin, 1998)

xx. http://lordshiprec.org.uk

xxi. http://www.berniegrantcentre.co.uk

xxii. William Robinson, 'The History and Antiquities of the Parish of Tottenham High Cross' 1818; Robinson vol 2, pp 1-87; Hall 1861, esp. pp 30-32